Developing Science

DEVELOPING SCIENTIFIC SKILLS AND KNOWLEDGE

ONE WEEK

year

2

Christine Moorcroft

A & C BLACK

Contents

Forces and movement

Using electricity

Published 2004 by A & C Black Publishers Limited
37 Soho Square, London W1D 3QZ
www.acblack.com

ISBN 0-7136-6641-2

Copyright text © Christine Moorcroft, 2004
Copyright illustrations © Kirsty Wilson, 2004
Copyright cover illustration © Kay Widdowson, 2004
Editor: Jane Klima
Design: Susan McIntyre

The author and publishers would like to thank Catherine Yemm, Trevor Davies and the staff of Balsall Common Primary School for their assistance in producing this series of books.

A CIP catalogue record for this book is available from the British Library.

Printed in Great Britain by St Edmundsbury Press Ltd, Bury St Edmunds, Suffolk.

A & C Black uses paper produced with elemental chlorine-free pulp, harvested from managed sustainable forests.

Introduction

Developing Science is a series of seven photocopiable activity books for science lessons. Each book provides a range of activities that not only develop children's knowledge and understanding of science, but also offer opportunities to develop their scientific skills: planning experimental work, and obtaining and considering evidence.

The activities vary in their approach: some are based on first-hand observations, some present the findings of investigations for the children to analyse and others require the children to find information from books and electronic sources. They focus on different parts of a scientific investigation: questioning, responding to questions, generating ideas, planning, predicting, carrying out a fair test or an investigation, recording findings, checking and questioning findings, explaining findings and presenting explanations.

The activities in **Year 2** are based on Science in the National Curriculum and the QCA scheme of work for Year 2. They provide opportunities for the children to:
- develop curiosity about the things they observe and experience, and explore the world with all their senses;
- use this experience to develop their understanding of key scientific ideas and make links between different phenomena and experiences;
- begin to think about models to represent things they cannot directly experience;
- try to make sense of phenomena, seeking explanations and thinking critically about claims and ideas;
- acquire and refine the practical skills needed to investigate questions safely;
- develop skills of predicting, asking questions, making inferences, concluding and evaluating (based on evidence and understanding), and use these skills in investigative work;
- practise mathematical skills such as counting, ordering numbers, measuring using standard and non-standard measures and recording and interpreting simple charts;
- learn why numerical and mathematical skills are useful and helpful to understanding;
- think creatively about science and enjoy trying to make sense of phenomena;
- develop language skills through talking about their work and presenting their own ideas, using systematic writing of different kinds;
- use scientific and mathematical language (including technical vocabulary and conventions) and draw pictures, diagrams and charts to communicate scientific ideas;
- read non-fiction and extract information from sources such as reference books or CD-ROMs;
- work with others, listening to their ideas and treating these with respect;
- develop respect for evidence and evaluate critically ideas which may or may not fit the evidence available;
- develop a respect for the environment and living things and for their own health and safety.

The activities are carefully linked with the National Literacy Strategy to give the children opportunities to develop their reading skills in finding information (for example, scanning a text, reading instructions and making notes) and to use a range of writing skills in presenting their findings (for example, labelling diagrams and writing simple reports). Science-related vocabulary to be introduced is listed in the **Notes on the activities** on pages 5–11.

Teachers are encouraged to introduce the activities presented in this book in a stimulating classroom environment that provides facilities for the children to explore through play, using movement and the senses. For example, you could provide an activity corner where the children can investigate materials, equipment, pictures and books connected with the topics to be covered (such as simple circuits and different materials), or you could use role play or PE lessons to explore movements (such as pushing and pulling).

Each activity sheet specifies the learning outcome and has a **Teachers' note** at the foot of the page, which you may wish to mask before photocopying. Expanded teaching notes are provided in the **Notes on the activities**. Most activity sheets also end with a challenge (**Now try this!**) that reinforces the children's learning and provides the teacher with an opportunity for assessment. These extension activities might be appropriate for only a few children; it is not expected that the whole class should complete them. They should be completed in a notebook or on a separate sheet of paper.

Health and safety

Developing Science recognises the importance of safety in science lessons and provides advice on and examples of the ways in which teachers can make their lessons as safe as possible (including links to useful websites). The books also suggest ways in which to encourage children to take appropriate responsibility for their own safety. Teachers are recommended to follow the safety guidelines provided in the QCA scheme of work or in *Be Safe!* (available from the Association for Science Education). Specific health and safety advice is included in the **Notes on the activities** and warnings to the children feature on the activity sheets where relevant.

Online resources

In addition to the photocopiable activity sheets in this book, a collection of online science resources is available on the A & C Black website at www.acblack.com/developingscience. These activities can be used either as stand-alone teaching resources or in conjunction with the printed sheets. An **ICT** icon on an activity page indicates that there is a resource on the website specifically designed to complement that activity.

To enable them to be used by children of a wide range of abilities, all the activities on the website feature both written and spoken instructions. The tasks have been designed to provide experiences that are not easy to reproduce in the classroom: for example, children can observe the seeds of unfamiliar plants, classify a collection of animals and sort rubbish.

These notes expand upon those provided at the foot of the activity pages. They give ideas for making the most of the activity sheet, including suggestions for the whole-class introduction, the plenary session or for follow-up work using an adapted version of the sheet. To help teachers to select appropriate learning experiences for their pupils, the activities are grouped into sections within each book, but the pages need not be presented in the order in which they appear, unless stated otherwise.

Where appropriate, links to other areas of the curriculum are indicated, in particular literacy and numeracy, and stories, songs, rhymes, jingles and poems are sometimes suggested for introducing the activities or for rounding them off.

Health and growth

This section builds on **Ourselves** and **Plants** from **Year 1**. The children learn from these activities that animals (including humans) grow and reproduce, and about some of the ways in which we can stay healthy.

All kinds of food (page 12) focuses on the need for food and drink in order to stay alive and healthy. You could introduce the activity with the cautionary tale of *Augustus who would not eat any soup* by Heinrich Hoffmann. (Enter 'Augustus + soup' in an Internet search or try the websites below.)
www.naughtykitty.org/augustus.html
www.fln.vcu.edu/struwwel/kaspar_e.html
www.strangelove.net/~kieser/Poetry/augustus.html
www.soupsong.com/iaugustu.html
Ask the children if the poem could have been about a real boy. What happens to people if they do not have enough to eat and drink? Ask the children what kinds of soup Augustus might have liked and what kinds he might not have liked. What other kinds of foods do people need?

> **Vocabulary:** *diet, drink, fish, food, fruit, meat, variety, vegetable, water.*

Sandwiches (page 13) allows the children to think and talk about the foods they like. In a mathematics lesson you could help the children to make a block graph on which to record the sandwich they like best out of those shown. The children could also conduct a survey to find out what the class would choose for a sandwich filling if they could have anything they liked. They could plan a picnic to provide something for everyone. Ask the children if they know what it means if someone is a vegetarian. What does he or she eat? Point out that, although the word sounds rather like *vegetable*, vegetarians do not eat only vegetables; they do not eat meat or fish (which involve killing the animals), but they might eat other foods from live animals such as cheese, eggs or milk. You could combine this activity with work in geography, visiting a farm, and in religious education, discussing the significance in some religions of specific meals and diets.

> **Vocabulary:** *diet, dislike, favourite, like, variety, vegetable, vegetarian.*

The king's banquet (page 14) helps the children to distinguish between the kinds of foods we need and those that are treats and should not be eaten quite so often. You could link this with work in religious education on celebrations. The children could make a display of pictures of special foods eaten at celebrations such as Christmas, Divali, Holi, Id-ul-Fitr, Pesach and Purim. It is important not to suggest that any foods are bad, since children do not usually have a choice about what they eat at home, and if anything they eat frequently at home is deemed to be 'bad' this could cause problems. After this activity the children could plan and draw a labelled picture of their own banquet of 'treat foods', display their pictures and talk to the class about them. This is an opportunity to make links with PSHE (Healthy lifestyles).

> **Vocabulary:** *diet, everyday food, healthy, treat, unhealthy.*

What moves? (page 15) draws the children's attention to what happens to their bodies while they are exercising. It builds on earlier work on the names of parts of the body. The children might wonder why the word *trunk* is included. Point out that it does not mean an elephant's trunk and show them the part of the body to which it refers. The sheet could be introduced through an activity song such as *One finger one thumb keep moving*, to which the children could add their own verses. This could be linked with literacy work on verbs.

> **Vocabulary:** *exercise, movement, stretch, trunk.*

Exercise (page 16) is about the effects of exercise on the body (change of skin colour, increased heart rate, sweat/perspiration and aching muscles – or an awareness that they have been exercised). For the extension activity information books and CD-ROMs will be needed. You could invite an exercise/fitness expert to talk to the children and answer questions about the effects of exercise on their bodies. They could explore this during PE lessons. Point out that the right kind and the right amount of exercise are good but that people can harm themselves by exercising too hard or too much.

> **Vocabulary:** *exercise, fitness, healthy, heartbeat, move, muscle, perspiration, skin, sweat, unhealthy.*

Growing and changing (page 17) concentrates on how people change as they get older. It builds on earlier work about increasing size. Here the children's attention is drawn to the fact that some older people are smaller  than some younger people. They could also cut pictures of people from magazines and clothing brochures and arrange them in order of age. PSHE lessons could be linked with this activity. If necessary, you could omit some of the pictures for some children.

> **Vocabulary:** *change, grow, growth, old, older, oldest, young, younger, youngest.*

Baby talk (page 18) discusses the sort of care babies need. It draws attention to the things a baby is able to do and the things other people have to do for it. The children could make a list of the things other people have to do for a baby. Display the list and invite the children to add to it when they think of something new. You could make a classroom display of the things babies need. Help the children to write labels for the items displayed. These could be checked during a literacy lesson.

Vocabulary: *care, help, older, toddler, younger.*

Marvellous medicine (page 19) introduces some of the ways medicines can help people who are ill. The children could first read *George's Marvellous Medicine* by Roald Dahl. Before beginning the activity sheet it is useful to show the children empty medicine bottles, packets and inhalers. Help them to read the words on the packets and ask them who should take these medicines and what for. Discuss the possible dangers of medicines and talk about the instances when the children should take medicines (only from a trusted adult). The questions to which the children could find answers include, for example, 'How do we become ill?', 'What different kinds of medicine are there?', 'What are medicines made of?' Link this with work in PSHE.

Vocabulary: *cure, lozenge, medicine, packaging, safe, safety, tablets.*

Dangerous doses (page 20) focuses on the dangers of misusing medicines, and can complement work in PSHE.
Suggested answers:
✗ because children should not take any medicine unless it is given to them by a trusted adult
✔ because the medicine has been prescribed by a doctor
✗ because medicines should be taken only by the person for whom a doctor prescribed them
✔ because the little girl's mum is giving her the medicine
✗ because medicines should be taken only for illnesses and when given by a trusted adult
✗ because even though the medicine was prescribed for the little girl, she should take it only when it is given by a trusted adult, except for routine medication such as inhalers for asthma, for which children can take responsibility. This could be discussed in PSHE lessons.

Vocabulary: *cure, dose, drug, medicine, safe, safety, tablets.*

Plants and animals in the local environment

The activities in this section help the children to learn about the plants and animals in their local environment and how different plants and animals are suited to different habitats. If the activities are undertaken during the spring, it is useful to grow some plants from seed: easy-to-grow plants include apple seeds, cress, marigolds, sunflowers and tomatoes. Avocado and orange seeds can be grown fairly easily if during germination the pots are placed inside a sealed plastic bag in a warm place.

Is it alive? (page 21) revises previous learning about living things and develops the children's understanding of the meaning of *alive*. You could begin by asking them to sort a set of objects (such as everyday classroom items, plants, insects and other small animals in appropriate containers) into two groups, labelled *alive* and *not alive*. Ask them how they can tell if something is alive. Explain why any animals shown are in containers and how you are looking after them (containers should have air-holes and some piece of vegetation or earth from the place where they were found, and the animals should be put back once they have been observed). To make the activity simpler, you could give clues, such as 'Does it breathe?', 'Does it need food?' During art lessons the children could make observational drawings of living things.

The children should wash their hands after handling plants or animals.

Vocabulary: *alive, animal, dead, living, not alive, plant.*

 Plant finder and **Animal finder** (pages 22–23) develop the children's understanding of the terms *alive* and *not alive*, *plant* and *animal*. Take them for a walk in the school grounds, a park or another safe place where they can see plants and animals. Can they find the ones on the activity sheets? What others can they find? Discuss how they can tell if something is a plant or an animal, and point out that people are animals. Discuss the meaning of the word *animal* and ensure that the children realise that animals include creatures such as worms, insects, spiders, snails, birds and fish. Discuss how to observe living things without harming them. Link this with English (poems and stories about plants or animals). A complementary activity for **Plant finder** is available on the website (see Year 2 Activity 1).

School and LEA guidelines should be followed for all visits, and teachers should check sites for harmful materials, e.g. dog faeces, glass, syringes. The children should always wash their hands after handling plants or animals.

Vocabulary: *alive, animal, dead, living, not alive, plant.*

 Seed time (page 24) develops understanding of the meaning of *flowering plant* and of how flowering plants reproduce. Some children might not realise that grasses are flowering plants: show them the flower parts and seeds. Introduce the names given to different kinds of seeds. Point out that nuts are seeds, but avoid having them in the classroom if any children are allergic (you could show pictures of familiar nuts such as Brazil nuts, cashew nuts, peanuts and walnuts). Red kidney beans should also be avoided because they are poisonous when raw. Seed collages could be made in art lessons. A complementary activity for this sheet is available on the website (see Year 2 Activity 2).

Check school and LEA health and safety guidelines and find out which plants are poisonous or irritant so that they can be avoided (see www.ntu.ac.uk/llr/library/poisonplantsguide.htm). The children should wash their hands after handling plants.

Vocabulary: *acorn, apple, broad bean, chestnut, conker, horse chestnut, nut, oak, peach, pip, stone, sweet chestnut, walnut.*

Plant a seed (page 25) reinforces understanding that plants grow from seeds and that seeds produce plants of the same kind as the one from which they came. It draws on children's previous learning about plants and provides an opportunity for teachers to assess their understanding of seeds and growth.

> **Vocabulary:** *germinate, plant, potting compost, seed, soil, sunlight, water.*

Is it fair? (page 26) introduces the concept of fair testing and helps the children to identify the factors that help a seed to germinate and grow. You could

 The children should wash their hands after handling plants and soil.

link this with literacy by reading the poem *Experiment* by Danielle Sensier (in *The Works 2*, Brian Moses & Pie Corbett, Macmillan). It is about an experiment to find out what plants need. Read the activity sheet with the children and ask them to describe how each seed is being treated. What differences are there between the treatment of the seeds? How will the children in the activity know if it is the light or something else that affects the growth of the seed? Draw out the need for comparing two seeds that are treated differently, why it is important to plant the same kinds of seeds in both pots and to change only the condition being investigated (light, water or soil/compost).

> **Vocabulary:** *condition, fair, germinate, grow, plant, seed.*

ICT This is your life (page 27) offers an opportunity for assessing the children's understanding of animal life cycles. Provide them with information books such as *The World of Ants* by Melvin Berger (Macmillan), *Amazing*

Eggs and *Change* (both in the Heinemann Discovery World series) and *Ants, Butterflies, Frogs, Rabbits* and *Sticklebacks* (all in the Picture Puffins Fact Book series). Discuss how the animal's life begins, the changes it goes through during its lifetime and the ability of adult animals to produce young by laying eggs or giving birth to live young. Introduce and explain the word *reproduce*. The children could draw pictures, write captions for them and then link them with arrows to indicate a life cycle. They could then rewrite this as a non-fiction recount (see *Developing Literacy: Non-fiction Year 2*, page 48). The children could also enact an animal's life story. A complementary activity for this sheet is available on the website (see Year 2 Activity 3).

> **Vocabulary:** *adult, birth, eggs, larva, reproduce.*

Variation

The activities in this section develop the children's awareness of the variety of living things (both animals and plants) and of the differences and similarities between them.

Animals and plants (page 28) reviews the children's understanding of the terms *animal* and *plant*. You could introduce this activity by asking the children to name an animal. Record their responses. If they name only mammals ask them if the following are animals: butterfly, frog, shark, snail and sparrow. Tell them that they are all animals, and name others, including humans. Ask them to name some plants. If they name only small pot and garden plants, ask them if the following are plants: apple tree, corn, grass, holly and sunflower. Tell them

that they are all plants, and name others.

> **Vocabulary:** *animal, ant, elm tree, goldfish, grass, horse, human, ivy, moss, plant, rose, seaweed, whale, worm.*

Animals alike (page 29) encourages the children to observe and think about animals. It could be carried out in conjunction with a visit to a farm, zoo or pet shop. Or you could provide some examples of live animals for the children to observe: for example, a snail, a goldfish or tropical fish, or a caged animal such as a hamster, gerbil or guinea pig; also observe any animals that can be seen around the school, including birds, pet animals and farm animals, depending on the neighbourhood (humans should also be observed). The children can write about observable features and what they know about animals: for example, they can all move around, they all breathe/need air, they all need water, they all feed/need food, they all produce young, they all grow. You could link this with work in geography on another country – finding out about the wildlife there and their habitats.

> **Vocabulary:** *air, alike, breathe, different, eat, feed, food, grow, humans, like, move, produce, same, similar, water, young.*

Human beings (page 30) focuses on the similarities between humans and reinforces the children's understanding that humans are animals. Possible answers include that all humans need air/breathe, eat, drink, grow, move around, talk and produce young.

> **Vocabulary:** *air, alike, animal, breathe, different, eat, food, grow, human, like, move, produce, same, similar, water, young.*

Guess who? (page 31) encourages close observation of detail. The children could colour the pictures to add to the differences between them. To play 'Guess who?' in pairs the children need two copies of the page: one kept intact and the other cut into separate cards. Player 1 has the intact page; Player 2 chooses a card, but does not show it to Player 1, who has to work out which person it is by asking questions to which the answer is *yes* or *no* (for example, 'Is it a boy?'). Player 1 covers the pictures that are eliminated until it is possible to work out which person Player 2 has chosen. As an extension activity the children could make their own version of the game using photographs of people they know.

> **Vocabulary:** *black, blond, curly, dark, eyes, fair, freckles, hair, long, medium, short, skin, straight.*

Plant talk: 1 (page 32) focuses on the ways in which plants are similar to one another. Possible answers include: 'We all grow', 'We all need water', 'We all need sunlight', 'We all produce seeds', 'We all die', 'We all have leaves', 'We all have flowers'. The children could copy and display their 'speech

bubbles': challenge the others to find plants to which the statements do not apply. This page and page 33 also support work in literacy on recording speech.

> **Vocabulary:** *alive, dead, die, flowers, leaves, roots, seeds, sunlight, water.*

Plant talk: 2 (page 33) focuses on the ways in which plants are different from one another. Encourage the children to describe the differences they can see. Possible answers include: 'My leaves are wider than yours', 'My leaves are pointed, but yours are rounded', 'My stem is thinner than yours', 'I have more flowers than you'. This activity also practises mathematical vocabulary.

> **Vocabulary:** *flowers, leaves, roots, seeds, stem.*

ICT Which flower? (page 34) encourages close observation of detail. The children should first colour the pictures, using plant information books for reference. Introduce words for describing flowers, such as *bell* and *trumpet*, and talk about the differences between the flowers. To play 'Which flower?' in pairs the children need two copies of the page: one kept intact, the other cut into separate cards. Player 1 has the intact page; Player 2 chooses a card, but does not show it to Player 1, who has to work out which flower it is by asking questions to which the answer is *yes* or *no* (for example, 'Is it red?'). Player 1 covers the pictures that are eliminated until it is possible to work out which flower Player 2 has chosen. As an extension activity, ask the children to make their own version of the game using photographs of plants. (You could help the children to photograph the plants in the school playground or in other local places.) A complementary activity for this sheet is available on the website (see Year 2 Activity 4).

> **Vocabulary:** *bell, colour, flower, leaf, shape, trumpet.*

Hand spans (page 35) focuses on measurable differences between people and can be linked with work in mathematics. It is more appropriate than measuring weight or height, about which some children might be sensitive, especially if they are overweight, underweight, very tall or very small. You could also ask the children to draw round the outlines of their outspread hands and their feet on coloured paper (plain or gift wrapping), cut out the hand shapes and display them. Another block graph could present the lengths of the children's feet. Ask them to write the names of their groups in order: shortest foot to longest foot. Are they in the same order as the hand spans? The children could also work in pairs to mark and cut strips of paper the same length as their height. Ask them to use cut-out outlines of their feet or hands to find out how many times their foot length or hand span fits into their height.

> **Vocabulary:** *block graph, centimetre, compare, hand span, length, measure, outspread, stretch.*

ICT Noah's ark (page 36) focuses on the ways in which animals can be grouped according to observable characteristics. You could begin by giving the children photographs or drawings of animals to sort in any way they like (working in pairs). Ask them to explain how they have sorted the animals: for example, whether or not they have wings, how they move, type of body covering. You could make copies of the ark outline to be split up and labelled differently. A useful poem about animal movements is *Jump or Jiggle* by Evelyn Beyer (see *Developing Literacy: Poetry Year 2*, pages 28 and 29). A complementary activity for this sheet is available on the website (see Year 2 Activity 5).

> **Vocabulary:** *feathers, fur, legs, movement, scales, skin, wings.*

Grouping and changing materials

The activities in this section develop the children's awareness of the different materials from which things can be made and of the meanings of *natural* and *made* or *non-natural*. They develop the children's understanding of the ways in which materials can be changed. It is essential to have available information books about natural and manufactured materials and their characteristics. Most of the activities in this section provide opportunities to make word-banks of adjectives.

ICT Rubbish collectors: 1 (page 37) revises learning about different types of materials and how to recognise them. It could be linked with the school's recycling schemes. The children could first sort a collection of samples of material (rather than objects) such as clay, fabric, metal, paper and plastic. Encourage them to name the materials (not the objects). A complementary activity for this sheet is available on the website (see Year 2 Activity 6).

The children should sort only 'rubbish' that has been carefully selected to avoid any harmful materials.

> **Vocabulary:** *clay, cotton, fabric, glass, material, metal, object, paper, plastic, wood, wool.*

Rubbish collectors: 2 (page 38) focuses on natural materials. You could begin by providing samples of natural materials such as bone, sheep's wool, wood, a piece of sheepskin or leather, sand, stone and clay. Introduce the word *natural*. Ask the children if they know where each of the materials comes from; point out that some natural materials come from plants, some from animals and some from the ground.

Bones should be sterilised and sheep's wool should be washed.

> **Vocabulary:** *bone, clay, cotton, fabric, iron, leather, material, natural, object, rubber, stone, wood, wool.*

Made materials (page 39) develops the children's awareness of the different materials that are made by mixing other materials. Collect and display objects made from manufactured materials. Use information books and pictures to help to explain simply how the materials are made (from natural materials): for example, glass is made from sand and silicon; steel is made by treating iron with carbon; plastic, polythene and nylon are made from petroleum; brass is a metal made by mixing copper with another metal – tin or zinc. Introduce the word *manufactured*.

> **Vocabulary:** *brass, glass, made, manufactured, material, mixture, natural, nylon, object, plastic, polythene, steel.*

Squashy, bendy, stretchy stuff (page 40) develops the children's awareness of the characteristics of materials and of the similarities and differences between the ways in which materials behave. Discuss the

Tin cans should have no sharp edges; soft drinks cans are best.

meanings of the words *squash*, *bend* and *stretch* and ask the children to demonstrate each action. They could predict whether or not an object can be squashed, bent or stretched and explain their predictions in relation to the material. Ask them to notice if each object goes back to its original shape. They could read poems about materials, such as those in *Out and About* by Shirley Hughes (Walker Books), and write some of their own.

> **Vocabulary:** *bend, material, object, squash, stretch.*

Heat changes (page 41) focuses on irreversible changes when materials are heated. Different groups (at different times) could observe each of the materials on the chart before and after heating.

 LEA and school guidelines should be followed for heating materials, and scrupulous hygiene should be observed so that the cake mix can be eaten once it has been baked. If the mixture contains eggs, do not let the children taste it uncooked.

> **Vocabulary:** *bendy, bigger, damp, dry, firm, hard, liquid, rigid, runny, slimy, sloppy, smaller, soft, solid, squashy, stiff, stretchy, wet.*

Cold stuff (page 42) focuses on a reversible change (melting ice). Prepare ice of different shapes and sizes: for example, ice cubes made in small, sectioned freezer trays, commercially-produced ice bags and balloons (which stretch when filled with water). Leave pieces of ice in dishes or bowls in the classroom during a break, so that the children can observe how it has changed when they return to the classroom. Ask them to notice which pieces of ice melt most quickly.

 The children should not touch ice straight from the freezer.

> **Vocabulary:** *cold, cool, cube, frozen, hard, icy, liquid, lukewarm, melt, melted, round, runny, shapeless, solid, water, wet.*

Meltdown (page 43) draws on personal experiences of ice and children's understanding of what makes ice melt. They should have noticed that small pieces of ice melt more quickly than large ones: they might suggest breaking the ice into small pieces; they might have noticed that ice lollies and ice creams melt quickly in hot weather: they might suggest heating the ice; they might have seen people putting salt on paths to melt the ice: they might suggest putting salt on it. Once the children have thought of a way to make ice melt more quickly, point out the need to compare this with leaving the ice on a dish in the classroom as in **Cold stuff**. Ask them if it would be fair to compare a huge ice balloon with a tiny ice cube, and discuss how they would be able to tell what made the ice melt quickly if they tried several ideas (for example, cutting it into small pieces, putting salt on it and heating it). If they have seen de-icer being used on car windscreens they might suggest using that, but this would be hazardous in school. In art lessons, the children could mix 'warm' and 'cold' colours.

 The children should not touch ice straight from the freezer.

> **Vocabulary:** *change, compare, fair, heat, hot, ice, melt, test, unfair, warm.*

Freeze it (page 44) focuses on the changes that happen to water and other liquids when they freeze. As in **Meltdown** it is important that the children can describe what they mean by *freeze* or *melt*. They could also predict what will happen when

other materials are put in a freezer. The activity draws on the children's experiences of ice at school and in everyday situations. They should know that water turns to ice when it is left in a freezer for long enough. They might also be able to comment on what makes water outdoors freeze. Ask them what happens to water when it turns to ice. How does it change? Use words such as *hard* and *solid* and ask the children to name other runny (*liquid*) materials that become solid when they are frozen. Draw attention to the fact that ice keeps its shape when it is taken out of a container. In literacy lessons you could focus on poems about ice and cold weather for a class anthology.

> **Vocabulary:** *change, freeze, frozen, hard, ice, liquid, melt, runny, solid, watery.*

Soft stuff (page 45) builds on the children's experiences of melting ice and develops their understanding of the different ways in which materials change when they are heated. They should notice that some materials need to be made hotter than others before they will soften. A safe way in which to soften all of the materials suggested is to put them into small plastic bags and place them in hot (not boiling) water. The children could also try placing the plastic bags on a radiator. Encourage them to feel the materials as well as to look at them before and after they have been heated in these ways. They could record their results on a simple comparison chart:

Material	What it looked like and felt like		Did it work?
	Before	After	
butter			
chocolate			
wax			

> **Vocabulary:** *change, feel, hard, heat, shape, soft, warm.*

Steam: 1 and **2** (pages 46–47) are about what happens to water when it is heated and then cooled. It demonstrates a reversible change, which can be compared with the irreversible changes the children observed in **Heat changes**. It is not necessary to introduce the words *reversible* and *irreversible* at this stage – but it is useful to point out that when ice changes to water and water to steam it is still water, whereas when some materials (for example, clay, cake mixture and eggs) are heated a new material is made. The activities support work in literacy (making labelled diagrams).

 These activities are for demonstration only. To keep the children safe it is useful to place a table between them and the surface on which the kettle is boiled and to wear an oven glove (pointing out the reason for these precautions).

> **Vocabulary:** *boil, boiling, bubbles, change, heat, hot, safe, steam, water.*

Forces and movement

The activities in this section develop the children's understanding of how pushes and pulls affect the shapes of objects and the ways in which objects move. You could link the work with literacy (describing words and words for actions) and collect poems about different kinds of movement.

All kinds of movement (page 48) reviews learning about different types of movement and about the words used for movements. It introduces the terms *push* and *pull* for forces. Before they begin the activity, take the children out to look for things in the local environment that move. Ask them to think of things that are not so obvious, such as leaves in the wind, a cat's whiskers, an eyelid. Ask them for verbs for the movements and ask if they can tell if the things are being pushed or pulled.

Vocabulary: *bend, pull, push, slide, squash, stretch, turn, twist.*

For **Shape-changers** (page 49) take the children on a tour of the inside and outside of the school to look for objects and materials whose shapes have

 School and LEA guidelines must be followed for work outside the school grounds.

been changed: for example, cars, gates and walls that have been hit by vehicles or other objects, elastic and fabrics that have been stretched, pastry that has been rolled out. Ask the children what caused the changes in shape. Was it a push or a pull?

Vocabulary: *bend, bump, crash, dent, flatten, force, pull, push, squash, stretch, turn, twist.*

Playtime (page 50) develops the children's awareness of what they have to do in order to make things move and to make them move faster, higher or further. Invite the children to read their answers aloud and ask the others if they have thought of anything

different. Draw attention to the forces used. Ask if they are pushes or pulls. Discuss the response of the children who completed the extension activity. What can they do to slow down a bike or scooter, to slow down when they are skating, to go down a slide more slowly or to make a swing slow down? Draw attention to the pushes and pulls. What is pushing or pulling? What is it pushing or pulling against? In a literacy lesson you could read the poem *The Swing* by Robert Louis Stevenson (in the *New Oxford Book of Children's Verse*, Oxford University Press).

Vocabulary: *far, fast, faster, force, further, furthest, hard, harder, high, higher, highest, move, push, strong, stronger, strongest.*

Speed up and **Slow down** (pages 51–52) develop children's awareness of the factors that affect speed of movement. It is not necessary to introduce the word *friction* at this stage but draw their attention to the surface on which the car is moving in page 51 and on which the marble is moving in page 52. Introduce the word *force* for *push*. In art lessons the children could look at the ways artists indicate speed: for example, Turner's *Rain, Steam and Speed*.

Vocabulary: *fast, faster, force, gentle, gently, hard, move, push, rough, slope, slow, slower, slowly, smooth, strong.*

What will happen? (page 53) develops the children's awareness of the factors that affect the distance something moves. Use the word *force* for *push*.

Vocabulary: *compare, distance, far, force, further, furthest, gently, height, high, higher, highest, move, push, ramp, slope.*

Race! (page 54) develops the children's awareness of the factors that affect the distance something moves. Use the word *force* for *push*. Help the children to identify the different factors that might affect the distance travelled by the vehicles: the height of the ramp, the size and shape of the vehicle, the floor surface (rough or smooth), how far up the slope it starts, how hard it is pushed. This is an opportunity to develop mathematical skills (measuring in non-standard and standard units).

Vocabulary: *compare, distance, far, force, further, furthest, gently, height, high, higher, highest, move, push, ramp, slope, surface, travel.*

Measuring up (page 55) focuses on fair testing and on recording and interpreting results. Discuss how the test is kept fair: the cars are all the same, they all start in

the same place, they all have a push of the same strength because they will be placed on the slope and allowed to roll, and the floor surface is the same for all of them. The only change is in the height of the slope. Before the children test the cars, encourage them to predict whether or not a high slope will make them travel further. What do they expect to see happening? Help them to measure the distances travelled (or some children could test the three cars side by side and compare the distances without measuring; they could record their results by drawing a picture to show the final positions).

Vocabulary: *compare, distance, far, force, further, furthest, height, high, higher, highest, measure, metres, ramp, slope, surface, travel.*

My investigation (page 56) focuses on how the children's ideas can be turned into questions to investigate and how the investigation or test can be made fair (by keeping all the factors that affect the movement of the cars the same and changing only the factor to be investigated: for example, floor surface, strength of push, shape of vehicle, size of vehicle, weight of vehicle). The strength of push can be tested by launching the cars along the ground using a piece of elastic fastened to the legs of two firmly anchored chairs (people can sit on the chairs to anchor them) and measuring the distance the elastic is pulled back to launch the cars. During another lesson you could help them to try out their ideas, to record their findings and to present these findings to the rest of the class. Encourage the others to check if the test was fair by noticing what has been changed. The children could contribute to a word-bank about forces.

Vocabulary: *change, compare, distance, fair, far, force, further, furthest, height, high, higher, highest, measure, metres, ramp, same, slope, surface, travel.*

Using electricity

It's electric! (page 57) introduces work on electricity. It helps the teacher to assess what the children understand about electricity and is an

 Children should not use electrical sockets at school, even if they are allowed to at home.

opportunity to point out the dangers of electricity. Ask the children if they know about any dangers of mains electricity: for example, it is dangerous to touch sockets with wet hands or to touch bare wires (there should not be any bare wires). Talk about the dangers of wires with frayed coating and of overloaded sockets. Also point out the covers of sockets not in use; explain why they should not be removed by the children and explain the dangers of poking things into sockets. Any mains electrical items in school should be checked regularly by an electrician. You could tell the children that this happens and show them the stickers that show when a check was last carried out.

Vocabulary: *danger, dangerous, electric, electrical, heat, light, mains, movement, plug, safe, safety, socket, sound, switch, wire.*

Mains or battery? (page 58) focuses on the difference between mains electricity and batteries. (Batteries have a much lower voltage. The

Children should not use electrical sockets at school, even if they are allowed to at home.

highest in everyday use is a car battery, which usually supplies 12 volts.) Tell the children that batteries are much less powerful than mains electricity and this is what makes them safe.

Never cut open batteries. Avoid rechargeable batteries except where they are enclosed in a device, and are not to be removed by the children. Do not let the children open devices such as watches and cameras, which contain small 'button' batteries.
Point out that it is safe to touch bare wires joined to batteries but that mains electricity is dangerous.

Vocabulary: *battery, danger, mains, powerful, safe.*

Keeping safe (page 59) develops the children's understanding of how to use electricity safely. Use it to review their previous

Point out that it is safe to touch bare wires joined to batteries but that mains electricity is dangerous.

learning (from pages 57–58). It could be linked with work in PSHE on personal safety.

Vocabulary: *battery, broken, check, cover, danger, electrician, frayed, mains, plug, powerful, safe, safety, socket, water.*

Circuit time (page 60) teaches children how to make a circuit using a battery, bulb and wires. You could also provide buzzers, which can be inserted in the circuit in place of the bulbs. Help the children to follow the path of the electricity around the circuit by pointing with a finger (from the battery, along the wire, through the bulb or buzzer and back to the battery). Where bulbs are used the children should also notice that it is important that the wires are connected to the right parts of the bulb:

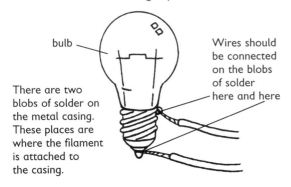
bulb
Wires should be connected on the blobs of solder here and here
There are two blobs of solder on the metal casing. These places are where the filament is attached to the casing.

You could link this activity with making decorations for religious celebrations such as Christmas and Divali.

Point out that it is safe to touch bare wires joined to batteries but that mains electricity is dangerous.

Vocabulary: *battery, bulb, connection, negative, positive, terminal, wire.*

ICT **What's wrong?** (page 61) focuses on the need for a circuit to be unbroken if it is to work. You could first show the children a picture of a bulb with wires attached to it but no battery. Ask them if the bulb will light, then let them test their ideas. Why did the bulb not light and what must they do to make it light? During the plenary session point out the need to make connections with both terminals of the battery (positive and negative). A complementary activity for this sheet is available on the website (see Year 2 Activity 7).

Vocabulary: *battery, broken, bulb, connection, join, negative, positive, terminal, wire.*

Check it (page 62) encourages the children to think about what they know about circuits and to use this understanding to work out where a problem lies in a faulty circuit. After the children have written their ideas, discuss how they can test them: for example, if they replace the bulb, battery and wire, how will they know where the problem was? Encourage them to discuss their ideas with a partner before writing and to say how they will know if each suggestion is the correct one. Then let them test the circuit and find out what was wrong.

Vocabulary: *battery, broken, bulb, connection, faulty, join, negative, positive, problem, terminal, wire.*

Make a quiz: 1 and **2** (pages 63–64) build on knowledge gained in the rest of this section. These pages encourage the children to solve a problem using a simple circuit. Before they begin, review their previous learning about circuits and show them how bulb-holders and battery-holders can be used to hold a circuit together. Point out how the electricity travels along the metal part of the battery-holder, along a wire to the bulb, along the metal part of the bulb-holder, through the bulb and back to the battery along the other wire. Ask the children why the ready-made circuit will not work as it is (it has a break in it). Once they have completed their quiz boards, ask the children how the quiz board can be used to complete the broken circuit (by connecting one wire to a paper fastener beside a question and the other to the paper fastener beside its answer). Can they explain why it does not work if the wrong answers are connected? This activity can be continued during a literacy lesson on writing questions and using question marks.

Vocabulary: *battery, break, broken, bulb, connect, connection, join, wire.*

All kinds of food

Recognise that there are many different foods

- **Sort the foods.**
- **Write the words in the sets.**

apple

tuna

chicken

carrot

sausage

potato

sardine

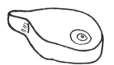
lamb chop

banana

pear

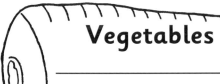

Fruit
_____
_____
_____

Vegetables
_____
_____

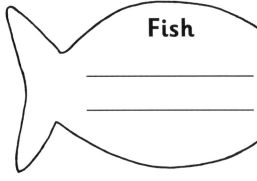

Fish
_____
_____

Meat
_____
_____

- **Think of another food in each set.**

Now try this!

- **Draw and label three drinks.**

Teachers' note Ask the children about a recent meal they have eaten. List the foods. Ask the children if they can see any foods in the list that are meat, fish, fruit and vegetables. Tell them that we need to eat different kinds of foods to stay healthy. Point out the importance of water. Can they think of any foods containing water?

Developing Science
Year 2
© A & C BLACK

Sandwiches

Understand that we eat different kinds of food

- **Ask your group which sandwich they like best.**
- **Write their names on it.**

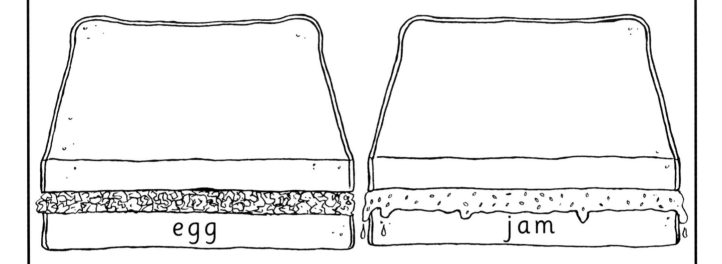

egg

jam

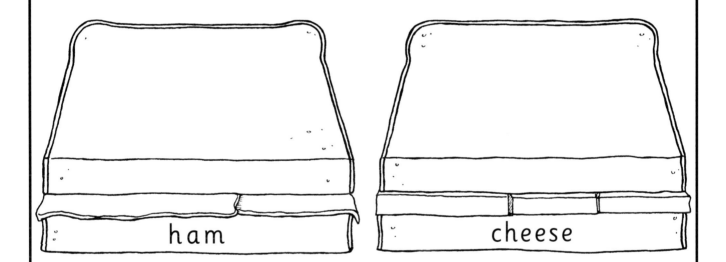

ham

cheese

Which is your group's favourite sandwich?

_____

Now try this!

- **List the** foods **you need to make your favourite sandwich.**

Teachers' note Ask the children about the foods they like. Can they eat whatever they like? Discuss the choices people sometimes have, and draw out that in families people can usually choose only a few of the foods they eat at mealtimes. Tell the children that in this activity they can choose from only four different sandwiches.

Developing Science
Year 2
© A & C BLACK

The king's banquet

Understand that we eat a lot of some foods and not very much of others

Which foods at the king's banquet are | treats |**?**

- **Colour them red.**
- **Colour the** | everyday foods | **green.**

turkey

naan

cola

star fruit

milk

fruit

rice

bread

mince pies

broccoli

water

cake

chips

salad

dates

jelly

cheese and biscuits

gingerbread men

Now try this!

- **Draw and label your favourite food** | treat |**.**
- **Draw and label your favourite** | everyday food |**.**

Teachers' note Introduce the words *everyday foods* and *treats*, and discuss their meanings. Ask the children to name foods they eat often and foods they are allowed only as a treat. Explain that we need more of some foods than others and that there are some foods, such as sweets and fizzy drinks, that we do not need at all, but that many people like.

Developing Science
Year 2
© A & C BLACK

What moves?

Recognise that we need exercise to stay healthy

Which parts of their bodies are the children moving?

What they are doing	Parts moved a lot	Parts moved a little
waving		
smiling		
jumping		
stretching		
throwing		
hopping		

Word-bank

arm	feet	hand	leg	mouth
arms	fingers	hands	legs	shoulder
eyes	foot	head	lips	trunk

Now try this!

- **Draw something you do in PE lessons.**
- **Label the parts that** move .

Teachers' note This could be linked with a PE lesson. Ask some of the children to carry out activities such as rolling, skipping and hopping while the others watch. Which parts of their bodies do they move? Introduce the word *exercise* and ask them which parts they exercised.

Developing Science
Year 2
© A & C BLACK

Exercise

Record simple observations

How do you feel after running and jumping?

• **Write in the boxes.**

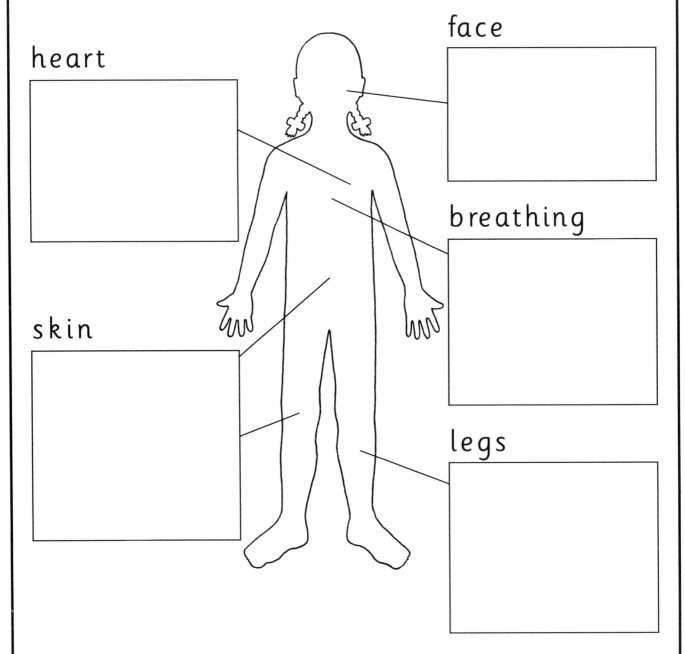

heart

face

skin

breathing

legs

Now try this!

Why do people shower and change their clothes after sports?

• **Write a sentence to explain.**

Teachers' note Before beginning the activity sheet the children need the opportunity to observe the changes that take place in their bodies after strenuous exercise such as running, skipping and hopping for five minutes or so. Ask them what happens to their skin, breathing and heartbeat. Can they feel anything in the muscles they have moved? (They should feel warm.)

Developing Science
Year 2
© **A & C BLACK**

Growing and changing

Understand that humans produce young and that children grow into adults

- ## Cut out the pictures.
- ## Put them in order [youngest] ——→ [oldest].

Teachers' note Show the children pairs of pictures of people of different ages and ask them who is the younger and who is the older and how they can tell. Point out that older people are not always bigger than younger ones and ask them for some examples among people they know. Give the children as many of the pictures on this page to sort as you think appropriate.

Developing Science
Year 2
© A & C BLACK

17

Baby talk

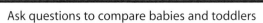

Ask questions to compare babies and toddlers

What can a [b a b y] **do?** ✔ **or** ✘
What can a [toddler] **do?** ✔ **or** ✘

	baby	toddler
suck		
drink from a cup		
walk		
sit		
talk		
cry		
read		
eat without help		

Now try this!

What else can a [baby] **do?**

• **Tell a friend.**

What else can a [toddler] **do?**

• **Write a sentence.**

Teachers' note If possible, invite a parent to bring in a baby and to talk to the children about what he or she has to do for the baby. Ask them about how babies in their own families are looked after. Show them a photograph of a baby and a toddler. Discuss the meaning of *toddler* and ask them which child is which. Discuss how each child needs to be looked after and the help he or she needs in doing everyday things.

Developing Science
Year 2
© **A & C BLACK**

Marvellous medicine

Ask questions about medicines

What do you want to know about medicines?

How can you find out?

Who can you ask?

What can you read?

What can you look at?

⚠ Only take medicine from an adult you trust.

My questions	Where I can find the answers	Answers

Now try this!

- **Find the answers to your questions.**
- **Write them on the chart.**

Teachers' note Ask the children about the times when they have taken medicine. What was it for? How did it help them and who gave it to them? Point out that some medicines can cure an illness and others just make people feel better. Encourage them to raise questions to which they can find the answers from books, electronic texts or a health professional invited to the school.

Developing Science
Year 2
© A & C BLACK

Dangerous doses

Understand that medicines are drugs, not foods, and can be dangerous

Should they take the medicines? or

I've got a headache.

Painfix for children

Time to take my tablet.

Mr B Jones Take 1 tablet every 4 hours

My stomach is aching.

Have some of this – it's from my doctor.

Mum. My throat is sore.

Have a throat lozenge.

Let's try these tablets.

I'm going to have some of my medicine.

Jane Lee Take 5ml 3 times a day

Now try this!

- **Write about a medicine you have taken.**

Or:

- **Draw a poster to warn children about the** dangers **of taking medicines.**

Teachers' note Introduce the word *prescription* and ask the children if they have heard it before. What do their parents or carers do with the prescription? Show them an empty bottle or package from a prescribed medicine and point out the name of the person for whom it was prescribed and the dose.

Developing Science
Year 2
© A & C BLACK

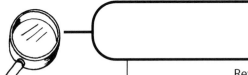

Is it alive?

- **Colour the things that are** $\boxed{\text{alive}}$.
- **Write labels for them.**

Word-bank

bird	grass
boy	spider
dog	squirrel
flower	tree

Now try this!

- **Draw three other things that are** $\boxed{\text{alive}}$.
- **Label your pictures.**

Teachers' note Ask the children what they know about living things: for example, what they do, what they need and how we should look after any living things we keep in school or at home. After the children have completed the activity, discuss the ways in which living things need to be looked after if they are kept in school.

Developing Science
Year 2
© A & C BLACK

Plant finder

- **Tick the** ⌷plants⌷ **you find.** ✔
- **Write their names.**

 Do not touch foxgloves – they are poisonous.

Word-bank

clover	foxglove
daisy	grass
dandelion	moss
fern	plantain

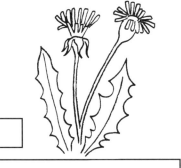

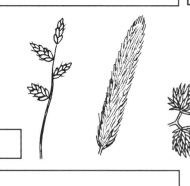

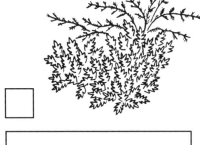

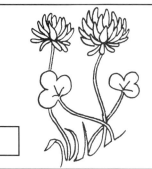

 Now try this!

- **Draw another** ⌷plant⌷.
- **Write its name.**

Teachers' note The children should first have completed page 21. Use this page in conjunction with page 23. Show the children some plants and cut flowers (alive and dead) in the classroom and ask them if they are alive and how they know. Take them to look for plants in the local environment. Look for the common plants on this page and keep a record of any other plants found. Ensure that the children realise that trees and grass are also plants.

Developing Science Year 2
© A & C BLACK

Animal finder

Observe and record animals found in the local environment

- **Tick the** animals **you find.**
- **Write their names.**

 Always wash your hands after touching animals.

Word-bank

ant	snail
butterfly	spider
centipede	woodlouse
slug	worm

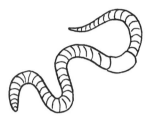

☐

☐

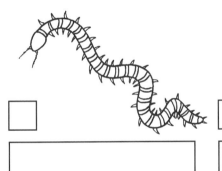

☐

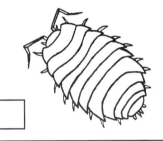

☐

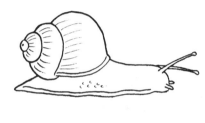

☐

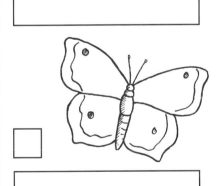

☐

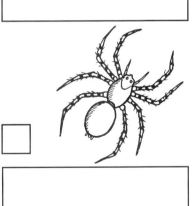

☐

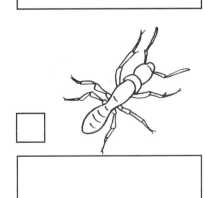

☐

Now try this!

- **Draw another** animal.
- **Write its name.**

Teachers' note The children should first have completed page 21. Use this page in conjunction with page 22. Show the children some pictures of animals (alive and dead) and ask them if they are alive and how they know. Take them to look for animals in the local environment. Look for the common animals on this page and keep a record of any other animals they find.

Developing Science
Year 2
© A & C BLACK

Seed time

- **Write the names of the** seeds.
- **Draw and name the** plant **that will grow from each seed.**

Seed	Plant
stone	

Word-bank

Seeds
acorn
conker
pip
stone

Plants
apple tree
horse chestnut
oak tree
peach tree

Now try this!

- **Draw and write about these seeds:**

walnut   broad bean   sunflower

Teachers' note Allow the children to observe the flowers and seeds of plants such as apples, avocados, beans, grass, honesty, horse chestnuts, oranges, peaches, peas and tomatoes. Tell them that these are flowering plants and that the seeds grow from the flowers. Talk about the names for different seeds. For the extension activity, have a walnut, a broad bean and a sunflower seed to show the children. Ask them to use information books about plants to find out what they will grow into.

Developing Science
Year 2
© A & C BLACK

24

Plant a seed

Understand that seeds produce new plants

- **Draw and write instructions for planting a** seed **.**

You need

1

2

3

4

Now try this!

- **Tell a partner about the things a plant must have so that it can grow.**

Teachers' note Discuss what the children know about planting seeds, show them some seeds and ask them to draw and label the things they need in order to plant the seed. What will they do to help it to grow? Introduce the word *germinate*. Ask them to use what they know to write instructions to help someone to plant a seed. If the children need help, you could display and label all the materials listed and ask them to look at the display.

Developing Science
Year 2
© **A & C BLACK**

Is it fair?

Here are four tests to find out how well seeds grow without light.

Are the tests ⎢fair⎥? ⎢yes⎥ or ⎢no⎥

dark cupboard   **sunny window ledge**

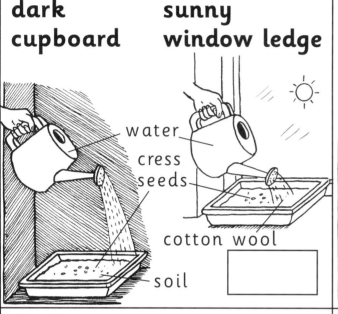

water
cress seeds
cotton wool
soil

dark cupboard   **sunny window ledge**

bean   sunflower seed
potting compost

dark cupboard   **sunny window ledge**

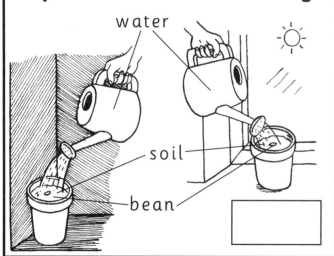

water
soil
bean

dark cupboard   **sunny window ledge**

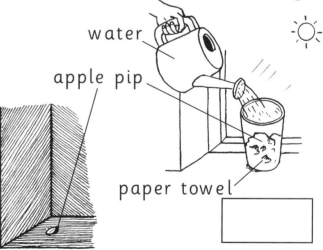

water
apple pip
paper towel

Now try this!

- **Draw and label a ⎢fair test⎥ to find out if a plant needs soil.**

Teachers' note The children should first have completed page 25. Ask them what is needed for a seed to grow. Would it grow if one of these conditions were missing? How can they find out? Discuss the need for a comparison between a seed that has all the conditions it needs and one that does not. If they change more than one condition (for example, by depriving the seed of both water and light), how will they know which one makes the difference?

**Developing Science
Year 2**
© A & C BLACK

This is your life

Understand that animals reproduce and change

- **Choose an animal.**
- **Tell the animal its life story.**

snail

butterfly

sheep

frog   hen

This is your life _____.

First of all you were _____.

After that _____

_____

_____

_____

_____

_____

_____

_____

Now try this!

- **Find out how long each stage in the animal's** life cycle **takes.**
- **Draw a chart.**

Teachers' note The children need access to information books in order to find out about the life cycle of an animal and how long each stage lasts (see the suggestions on page 7). Help them to make notes and then to write the animal's life story on this page.

Developing Science
Year 2
© A & C BLACK

Animals and plants

- **Cut out the pictures.**
- **Put them into sets:** $\boxed{\text{animals}}$ **and** $\boxed{\text{plants}}$.

ant

elm tree

goldfish

grass

horse

human

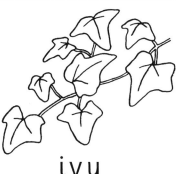

ivy

moss

rose

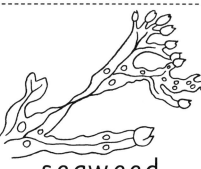

seaweed

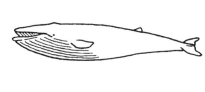

whale

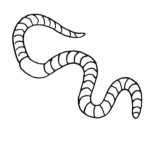

worm

Teachers' note Ask the children if all the things in the pictures are living things. Read the names of the animals and plants with them. After they have sorted the pictures, as an extension they could draw and label others to add to each set. Make a copy of this page with the pictures masked, so that they have cards of the right size.

Developing Science
Year 2
© A & C BLACK

Animals alike

Make careful observations of similarities between animals

How are the animals | alike |?

• **Write sentences.**

human

dog

rabbit

spider

frog

ladybird

stickleback

dolphin

They are all alive.

They can all _____.

They all need _____.

They all _____.

They all _____.

Now try this!

• **Draw another animal.**

How is it like these animals?

• **Write a sentence.**

Teachers' note Ask the children if all the pictures show animals. If they think any are not animals, ask them why. After they have completed the activity invite the children to read their sentences aloud while the others listen and check that they are correct. Challenge them to think of animals to which the sentences do not apply.

Developing Science
Year 2
© A & C BLACK

Human beings

How are humans alike?

- **Write sentences.**

They are all alive.
They all _____.
They _____.

_____.

_____.

_____.

_____.

Now try this!

How are humans different from other animals?

- **Write two sentences.**

Teachers' note Ask the children if all the animals in the picture are humans. How can they tell? Ask them about the ways in which humans are like one another but different from other animals. To simplify the activity, you could write some words to begin each sentence.

**Developing Science
Year 2
© A & C BLACK**

Guess who?

Explore human variation

Lee

Alice

Great-grandpa

baby

Gran

Dad

Mum

Guy

Auntie Kate

Moira

Ben

Sara

Teachers' note This page can be used as a logical guessing game played in pairs (see page 7), or as a 'Who am I?' game. For this each child takes a card and keeps it hidden; they then take turns to give information as if they are the person on their card: for example, 'I am a boy, but not a young one. I have short, fair hair. I have a round face.' The aim is to give a good enough description for the others to work out who it is.

Developing Science
Year 2
© A & C BLACK

Plant talk: 1

Understand that local plants have similarities

- Imagine that plants can talk about how they are alike.

What might they say?

We all ___ ___

apple tree

We all ___

grass

We all ___ ___

poppy

We all ___

daisy

We all have roots.

oak

What do all plants need?

- Draw a plant and write a speech bubble.

Now try this!

Teachers' note Ask the children if all the pictures show plants. If they think any are not plants, ask them why. After they have completed the activity invite the children to read their sentences aloud while the others listen and check that they are correct. Challenge them to think of plants to which the sentences do not apply. To support children who find this difficult, you could ask 'Does this plant have a stem?', 'Do the others have stems?' and so on.

Developing Science
Year 2
© A & C BLACK

32

Plant talk: 2

Understand that local plants have differences

- **Imagine these two plants can talk about how they are** different .
- **Write in the speech bubbles.**

- **Write another speech bubble for each plant.**

Teachers' note The children should first have completed page 32. Draw their attention to the shapes of the leaves and flowers, the width and length of the leaves, and the length and thicknesses of the roots and stems of the plants.

Developing Science
Year 2
© A & C BLACK

33

Which flower?

Make observations and comparisons of local plants

rose

apple blossom

dandelion

sunflower

daffodil

pansy

bluebell

poppy

daisy

thistle

foxglove

tulip

Teachers' note The children should first have completed pages 32–33. This page can be used as a logical guessing game played in pairs (see page 8), or as a 'What am I?' game. Ask them first to colour the flowers. Each child takes a card and keeps it hidden; they then take turns to give information as if they are the flower depicted: for example, 'I have big red petals with black parts in the centres, and a hairy stem.' The others should work out which flower it is.

Developing Science
Year 2
© **A & C BLACK**

Hand spans

Measure differences between themselves and other children

- **Measure your hand span.**

  [   ] centimetres

- **Record your group's hand spans on the chart.**

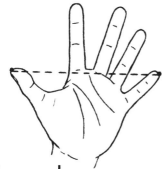

hand span

Name	Hand span in centimetres														
	6	7	8	9	10	11	12	13	14	15	16	17	18	19	20

- **Write your group's names in order.**

  [shortest hand span] _____

  ↑ _____

  _____

  _____

  _____

  [longest hand span] _____

Now try this!

- **Do the people with the longest hand spans have the largest feet? Find out.**

Teachers' note The children need rulers. Revise how to measure in centimetres and ask them if they know what a hand span is. Demonstrate a hand span and ask them if it is always the same length; discuss how they should measure it. The simplest way is to measure from the tip of the thumb to the tip of the little finger with the hand stretched as wide as possible.

Developing Science
Year 2
© A & C BLACK

Noah's ark

Group living things according to observable characteristics

Which animals can go in each room?
• Write their names.

2 legs only – first class

No legs allowed

8 legs here

6 legs here

4 legs only in here

Come here if you have too many legs to count.

Developing Science
Year 2
© A & C BLACK

Teachers' note Enlarge this sheet to A3 and give each group one copy. Ask the children to look at pictures of animals and to decide in which parts of Noah's ark they can go. Where will Noah and his family go? The children could look for other similarities (as well as differences) between the animals they have grouped by number of legs.

Understand that there is a range of materials with different characteristics

Rubbish can be made of different | materials |.

- **Think of things people throw away.**
- **List them in the shapes.**

I like metal rubbish.

nails
_____
_____
_____
_____

We like paper rubbish.

letters
_____
_____
_____
_____
_____
_____

I like plastic rubbish.

yogurt pots
_____
_____
_____
_____

I like fabric rubbish.

old socks
_____
_____
_____
_____

 Now try this!

- **Write a list of rubbish made from a different material.**

Teachers' note Point out that in this activity the children will write the names of objects that can be made from each of the materials. In the extension activity they could name objects made of stone, clay or glass. To help the children to distinguish between materials, provide a display of four labelled boxes of items made of the four materials.

Developing Science
Year 2
© A & C BLACK

Rubbish collectors: 2

What is the rubbish made of?

- **Write labels.**

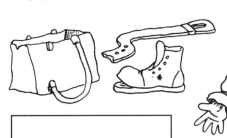

I collect natural rubbish.

Word-bank

bone
clay
cotton
iron
leather
rubber
stone
wood
wool

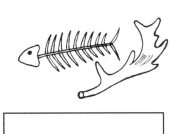

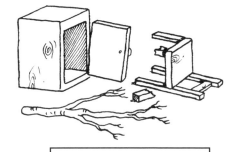

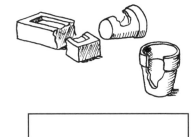

Now try this!

- **Draw and write three other things made from** natural materials **.**

Teachers' note The children should first have completed page 37. Ask them if they know where any of the materials they have observed come from. Do people make them or are they found and then shaped? Read the names of the materials in the word-bank and discuss where they come from: from plants, animals or the ground. Before beginning the activity, help the children to make and label a display of natural materials.

Developing Science
Year 2
© A & C BLACK

Made materials

Understand that some materials do not occur naturally

- **Look for objects made from materials that are not natural.**
- **On the screen, list the things you find.**

Made materials

brass	glass	nylon
_____	_____	_____
_____	_____	_____
_____	_____	_____
_____	_____	_____
plastic	**polythene**	**steel**
_____	_____	_____
_____	_____	_____
_____	_____	_____
_____	_____	_____

○ ○ ○   ○

Now try this!

- **Choose three of the** made materials .
- **Tell a friend about what each one is made from.**

Teachers' note The children should first have completed pages 37–38. They should also have the opportunity to observe and handle objects made from the materials featured on this page. Ask them how they know if an object is made of brass, glass or plastic. Discuss how they recognise other materials. To help the children, you could make a labelled display of 'made materials' (or pictures of them).

Developing Science
Year 2
© **A & C BLACK**

Squashy, bendy, stretchy stuff

Understand that objects or materials can be altered

Which objects can you ⬚squash⬚, ⬚bend⬚ or ⬚stretch⬚?
What are they made of?

Object	Can you squash it?	Can you bend it?	Can you stretch it?	What is it made of?
paper clip				
pencil				
ball				
ruler				
sock				
envelope				
can				

• **Draw and label three things that you can ⬚twist⬚.**

Teachers' note Provide the children with examples of the objects listed on the chart. Ask them to name the objects and then to name the materials from which they are made. They should test each object in turn and record their findings on the chart.

Developing Science
Year 2
© A & C BLACK

Heat changes

Understand that materials often change when they are heated

What are these materials like before and after they are heated?

Can they be changed back to how they were?

Word-bank

bendy	slimy
bigger	sloppy
damp	smaller
dry	soft
firm	solid
hard	squashy
liquid	stiff
rigid	stretchy
runny	wet

Material	Before heating	After heating	Can it be changed back?
clay 			
egg			
cake mix			
bread dough			

Teachers' note Encourage the children to describe the materials before they are heated, using adjectives such as those listed. Introduce words such as *firm*, *rigid* and *liquid*. Draw the children's attention to the shape and size of the material before and after heating, what it feels like and its colour.

Developing Science
Year 2
© A & C BLACK

41

Cold stuff

Explore melting ice using appropriate senses

What will happen to ice if you leave it in the classroom?

_____

- **Record the changes on this chart.**

Before		After	
What it looked like	What it felt like	What it looked like	What it felt like

Word-bank

cold
cool
cube
frozen
hard
icy
liquid
luke warm
melt
melted
round
runny
shapeless
solid
water
wet

Now try this!

- **Can you change the melted ice back?**
- **Write and draw what you can do.**

Teachers' note Ask the children to describe the ice: what it feels like, its shape, colour, texture and size. What do they think will happen to the ice if it is left in the classroom? If they say that it will melt, ask them what happens when ice melts. How can they tell when an ice cream or ice lolly melts? Draw out that when something hard (solid) melts it becomes runny (liquid).

Developing Science
Year 2
© A & C BLACK

Meltdown

Use knowledge about what makes ice melt to plan what to do

How can you make ice melt more quickly?

- **Draw and write in each box.**

This is what we shall do:

We shall need these things:

This is what we think will happen:

This is how we shall know if it worked:

Teachers' note The children should first have completed page 42. Discuss what makes ice melt, and ask them to think of a way to make a piece of ice melt as quickly as possible; they should fill in the first part of the chart. Discuss how to make tests fair (see page 9). If their idea works, what will they expect to see? (The ice tested should melt more quickly than that left on a dish in the classroom.) If the children find this difficult, it could be completed as a group activity led by an adult.

Developing Science
Year 2
© **A & C BLACK**

43

Freeze it

Recognise that many materials change when they are cooled

Ali and Lisa are trying to make a striped ice lolly, like this:

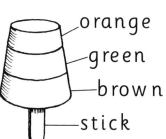

orange
green
brown
stick

- **Read their plans.**
  Will they work? ☑ **or** ☒
  Why or why not?

Ali: I'm going to put orange juice, then lime juice, then cola into a pot and then put it in the freezer.

☐ Reason _____
_____
_____
_____
_____
_____

Lisa:

Put some orange juice in a pot.
Leave it to freeze.
Pour in some lime juice.
Put it back in the freezer.
When it has frozen, pour in some cola.
Leave it to freeze.

☐ Reason _____
_____
_____
_____
_____
_____

Now try this!

How do things change when they freeze ?

- **Draw and write about:**

water   soup   bread

Teachers' note The children should first have completed pages 42–43. Ask them to predict what will happen when water is put into a freezer. Will the same happen to fruit juices and fizzy drinks? Encourage them to use what they know about ice to decide whether each method of making a striped ice lolly will work. They could try making striped ice lollies with ingredients of their choice.

Developing Science
Year 2
© **A & C BLACK**

Soft stuff

How can hard **materials be made** soft **?**

- **Write what you will do.**
- **Write what happens.**

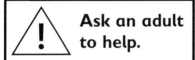
⚠ **Ask an adult to help.**

Material	What I shall do	What will happen
butter		
chocolate		
wax		

Now try this!

- **Share your results with other groups.**

  What was the best way of making each material soft?

  Why?

Teachers' note The children should first have completed pages 42–44. Provide samples of butter, chocolate and candle wax for them to look at and handle. Ask them to describe the appearance and feel of the materials. How can they be made soft? Discuss safe ways of heating the materials and ask the children to write what they will do to soften the materials and what they think will happen. Help them to try out their ideas and then to record them on a chart.

Developing Science
Year 2
© A & C BLACK

Steam: 1

- **Label the picture.**
- **Write what happens.**

  How does the water change?

⚠ **Be careful! Hot water and steam can burn your skin.**

Word-bank

boil	hot
boiling	hotter
boils	kettle
bubbles	steam
changes	water

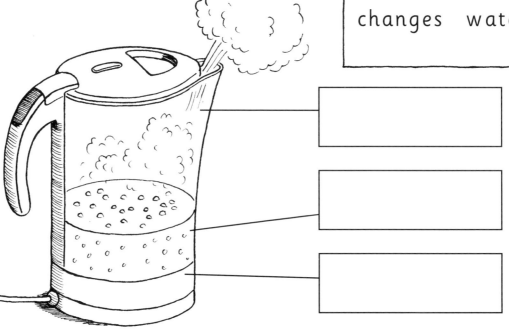

_____

_____

_____

Now try this!

- **Write what will happen if the water is left to** `boil` **for a long time.**

Teachers' note Tell the children that they are going to watch carefully and then describe what happens when water is heated. Boil some water in a kettle or pan and ask the children what they can see happening. If they say that the water is boiling, ask them what they can see happening when it boils. What can they see coming from it? What is steam made of? Follow up this activity with page 47.

Developing Science
Year 2
© **A & C BLACK**

46

Understand that on cooling the steam turns back to water

- **Watch what your teacher does.**
- **Label the picture.**
- **Write what happened.**

How did the steam **change?**

 Hot water can burn you – take extra care.

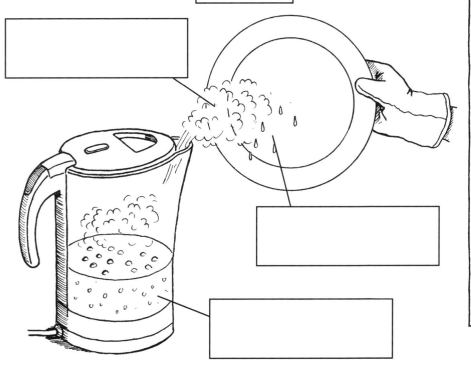

Word-bank

boils
changes
cold
cools
drops
hot
run
steam
water

_____

_____

_____

_____

_____

 Now try this!

Why do kitchen windows sometimes steam up?

- **Tell your partner about what happens.**

Teachers' note The children should first have completed page 46. Boil a kettle again and ask the children what they can see coming from it. What is steam made of? Hold a cold plate near to the steam and then hand the plate to the children so that they can feel it. What is on the plate? Where did the water come from? How did it get there? You could continue to boil the water (in a non-automatic kettle) so that the children can see that there is less water in it than at the start.

Developing Science
Year 2
© A & C BLACK

All kinds of movement

- **Match the words to the movement.**
- **Write the words.**

Word-bank
bend
slide
squash
stretch
turn
twist

Now try this!

- **Draw a picture in which a dog is** pulling **.**
- **Draw a picture in which a dog is** pushing **.**

Teachers' note Discuss the pictures and read the words on the word-bank with the children. You could invite some volunteers to demonstrate each movement. Ask them to write one of those words in each box to show how the cat is moving. Afterwards, invite the children who complete the extension activity to read their answers aloud and ask the others to comment.

Developing Science
Year 2
© A & C BLACK

Shape-changers

Recognise that sometimes pushes or pulls change the shape of objects

How can you change the shape of things?

Can you push them or pull them,
or both?

Draw and write in the boxes.

Material	How I can change its shape	
	Pushing	**Pulling**
sand		
dough		
sponge		
rubber		

Now try this!

- **Try changing the shapes of other materials.**
- **Draw and write about what you did.**
- **Use the words push and pull.**

Teachers' note Provide the children with the materials shown and let them experiment with changing their shapes. Which ones can they pull and which can they push? They should record their findings on the chart. The children who complete the extension activity could make another chart on which to record their findings.

Developing Science
Year 2
© A & C BLACK

Playtime

Explain how to make familiar objects move faster or more slowly

How can these children go $\boxed{\text{faster}}$ or $\boxed{\text{higher}}$?

- **Draw and write about what they can do.**

bike		_____ _____ _____
scooter		_____ _____ _____
skates		_____ _____ _____
slide		_____ _____ _____
swing		_____ _____ _____

How can they $\boxed{\text{slow}}$ down?

- **Draw and write about your ideas.**

Teachers' note Ask the children about their experiences of playground items such as swings, slides, seesaws and round-abouts, and moving toys such as bikes, scooters and skates. What do they do to go faster, higher or further? They could tell the story of how they have done this (for example, making a swing go as high as possible).

Developing Science
Year 2
© A & C BLACK

Explain how to make familiar objects move faster

How can Amy make the car go ⏹️faster⏹️?

• Draw and write about what Amy could do.

[ ]

Amy could _____

_____

_____

_____

_____

Why do you think your idea will work?

Now try this!

Teachers' note The children should first have completed page 50. Ask them to investigate ways of making a toy car move quickly along the floor and then to look at the picture and to say what is stopping the car from going fast. What can be done about it? What else can Amy do? In addition to using a smooth floor surface, she could push the car harder, roll it down a ramp or launch it using a long piece of elastic fastened to something firm. Discuss the children's ideas.

Developing Science
Year 2
© **A & C BLACK**

How can James make the marble roll more slowly ?

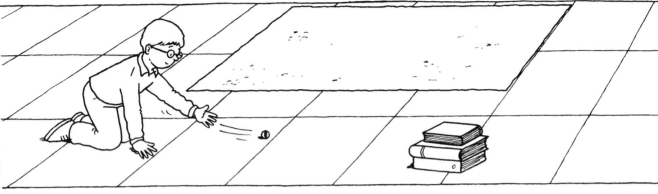

• Draw and write about what James could do.

James could _____

_____

_____

_____

Why do you think your idea will work?

Now try this!

Teachers' note The children should first have completed pages 50–51. Ask them to roll a marble along the floor and then to look at the picture and to say what could be done to slow down the marble. James could push the marble more gently, use a rough floor surface or arrange the books at angles so that a rolling marble hits a book, rolls alongside it, hits another book and so on. The angles of the books and the distances between them will affect the speed of the marble.

Developing Science
Year 2
© **A & C BLACK**

What will happen?

- **Look at the pictures.**

  Which car will go the **?** ☑

  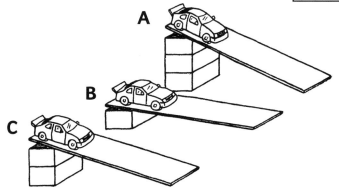

  ☐

  ☐

  ☐

  What will make that car win? _____

  _____

  _____

  What will happen?

- **Draw where the cars will finish. Label them.**

What could you do to make the cars go even further**?**

Teachers' note The children should first have completed pages 50–52. Ask them to describe what they see in each picture. What is the only difference between them? The children should look at the heights of the ramps to estimate which will go furthest. They should draw the cars in first, second and third places at the end of the 'race' in order of distance covered. Ask them what they think will make the cars go further.

Developing Science
Year 2
© **A & C BLACK**

Race!

Evaluate whether a test was fair

Sam, Jo and Raj are finding out if a higher slope makes a car go further.

truck

block

slope

smooth floor

car

blocks

slope

carpet

push

car

blocks

slope

smooth floor

List the things that stop the test being fair:

_____

_____

_____

_____

_____

Now try this!

• **Draw and label a** | fair test | .

Teachers' note The children should first have completed pages 50–53. Ask them what is similar about each picture and what is different. What might make the cars travel further? How could they find out? How would they be able to tell which of these things was making the difference?

Developing Science
Year 2
© A & C BLACK

Measuring up

Make measurements and record them in a table

• Colour the boxes to show how far the cars travel.

Car

A													
B													
C													

Which car went the furthest? _____

What made it go a long way? _____

What could you do to make the car go even further?

Now try this!

Teachers' note The children should first have completed pages 50–54. Ask them how the test has been made fair. Provide them with the materials shown in the picture and a long tape measure. Let them test three identical toy cars on slopes as depicted and talk about how the test is being kept fair (see page 10). Ask the children to think what else might make the cars go further, and how they could test it. The scale on the chart has been omitted so that it can be adapted as required.

Developing Science
Year 2
© A & C BLACK

My investigation

Suggest a question to test and predict what will happen

How can you test your idea for making a car go further?

My question:

This is what I shall do:

Draw and write.

I shall need these things:

_____

_____

_____

_____

I shall keep these things the same:

I shall change only this:

This is what I think will happen:

Now try this!

- **Carry out your test.**
- **Write what happened.**

Teachers' note The children should first have completed pages 50–55. Ask them to think of one of the other factors they have talked about which affects how far a car travels. Help them to express this as a question and ask them to talk to a partner about what they could do (see page 10). They can plan their investigation with a partner or a small group. What do they think will happen? How will they know the answer to their question?

Developing Science
Year 2
© **A & C BLACK**

It's electric!

- **Look for** electrical **things at school. What do they do?**
- **Draw and label the electrical things.**

Do not touch electric sockets.

These give light	These give heat
These make sounds	**These make things move**

Now try this!

- **Draw and write about another electrical thing.**

  What does it do?

Teachers' note Take the children for a walk around the school to find things that are worked by electricity. Discuss what electricity makes the things do. Encourage them to observe light, heat, movement and sound. A simpler activity would be to show the children electrical appliances and ask 'Does it give light?', 'Does it give heat?' and so on. They could label some of them with removable stickers: 'light', 'heat', 'sound' or 'movement'.

Developing Science
Year 2
© A & C BLACK

Mains or battery?

Do these work from `mains` electricity or from a `battery`?

 ⚠ **Mains electricity can be dangerous.**

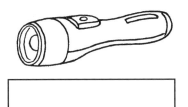

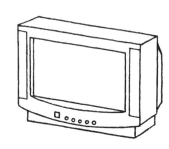

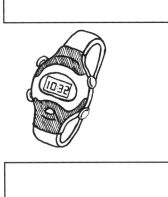

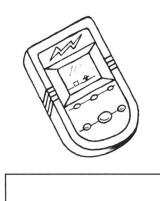

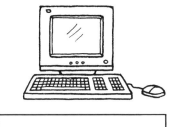

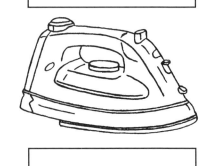

Now try this!

- **Draw something else that works from a `battery`. Label your picture.**
- **Draw something else that works from `mains` electricity. Label your picture.**

Teachers' note Show the children a collection of devices that work from batteries and some that work from the mains: for example, a torch, a flashlight, a hand-held computer game, a wristwatch, an electric kettle, an electric iron, a television set and a computer. Let them investigate the connections of a battery in a torch. Point out that batteries are safe; we can safely touch bare wires that are connected to small batteries of this kind.

Developing Science Year 2 © A & C BLACK

Keeping safe

Understand that everyday appliances are connected to the mains

• **Write some rules for using** $\boxed{\text{mains}}$ **electricity.**

Do

_____

_____

_____

_____

_____

Do not

_____

_____

_____

_____

_____

_____

Now try this!

• **Write notes about the differences between** $\boxed{\text{mains}}$ **electricity and** $\boxed{\text{batteries}}$ **.**

Teachers' note The children should first have completed pages 57–58. Use this page to assess their understanding of the danger of mains electricity and how this is different from battery power. For children who need more support, this could be carried out as a group activity led by an adult.

Developing Science
Year 2
© A & C BLACK

59

Circuit time

Make a complete circuit using a battery, wires and a bulb

What can you do to make this small bulb light up?

bulb

You could use

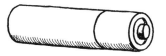

battery   wires   sticky tape

• **Make your** circuit **.**

• **Draw and label the circuit.**

Does the circuit work?

Now try this!

• **Make a circuit with a buzzer.**

• **Draw and label the circuit.**

• **Test it.**

Teachers' note Provide the children with a battery, some pieces of wire and a bulb. Do not provide bulb-holders at first because these stop the children from seeing the connections. Ask them to see if they can make the bulb light and to demonstrate how their circuit works. Use sticky tape to hold all the pieces in place. Point out the two poles of the battery and introduce the words *positive*, *negative* and *terminals*.

Developing Science
Year 2
© A & C BLACK

Make and test predictions about circuits

Will the bulbs light?

- **Predict, then test the** | circuits |.

1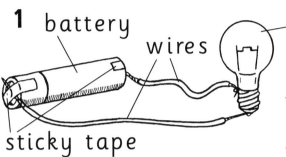
battery
wires
bulb
sticky tape

Will the bulb light?

Were you right?

2
battery
wires
bulb
sticky tape

Will the bulb light?

Were you right?

3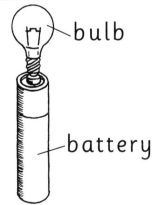
bulb
battery

Will the bulb light?

Were you right?

Now try this!

- **Investigate the bulbs that did not light.**

  How can you make them light?

- **Draw and write about what to do.**

Teachers' note The children should first have completed page 60. This activity focuses on the need for a complete, unbroken metal circuit. Review the children's previous learning about making a circuit, stressing the necessity for it to be unbroken. After they have answered the questions, ask them to explain why each circuit will not work, before giving them the materials with which to test it.

Developing Science
Year 2
© A & C BLACK

Check it

Make and test predictions about circuits that will not work

This bulb will not light.

bulb

bulb-holder

wires

sticky tape

battery

What might be wrong?

Write two or three ideas.

1 _____

2 _____

3 _____

How can you test each idea?

1 _____

_____

_____

2 _____

_____

_____

3 _____

_____

_____

Now try this!

- **Test more circuits that do not work.**
- **Fix them and write about what you did.**

Teachers' note The children should first have completed pages 60–61. Ask them to complete the first part of the activity before giving them the circuit to check. You could ask some children to write two ideas and others to write three: the bulb might not be working, the battery might be dead or one of the wires might have a break inside it.

Developing Science
Year 2
© A & C BLACK

Recognise that circuits can be used to make simple devices

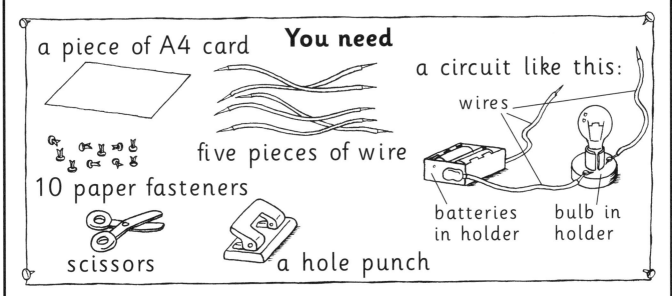

You need

a piece of A4 card

five pieces of wire

10 paper fasteners

scissors

a hole punch

a circuit like this:

wires

batteries in holder

bulb in holder

- **Cut out the quiz and glue it on the card.**

- **Punch 10 holes in the quiz card and push paper fasteners through the holes.**

- **On the back, join the questions to the right answers by wrapping the ends of the wires round the fasteners:**

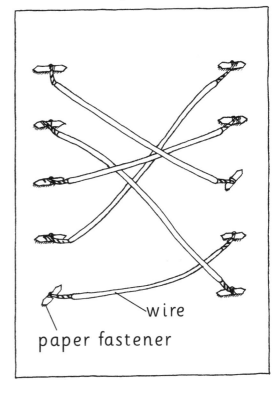

back of quiz

wire

paper fastener

Now try this!

- **Find a way to use the circuit to check if people give the right answers.**

Teachers' note Use this with page 64. Show the children the quiz on page 64 and read the questions with them. Ask them to find the answers. After they have glued the quiz on to a piece of cardboard, show them how to punch holes in the cardboard and how to fix the paper fasteners through the holes. Continued on page 64.

Developing Science
Year 2
© **A & C BLACK**

Make a quiz: 2

Recognise that circuits can be used to make simple devices

○	What is the name for a young cow?	six	○
○	Which animal has fur and can fly?	foal	○
○	How many legs does a butterfly have?	bat	○
○	How many legs does a spider have?	calf	○
○	What name is given to a young horse?	eight	○

Teachers' note Use this with page 63. Ask the children to join the questions to the right answers using pieces of wire. Give them the ready-made circuit and then ask them to work out how they can use the circuit to show if someone has given the right answer.

Developing Science
Year 2
© A & C BLACK